Ideas & Inspiration for

Family Fun Nights

Stirring Up Fun Together

FAMILY SERIES

Printed in the United States of America
by G&R Publishing Company

Distributed by:

 Products

507 Industrial Street
Waverly, IA 50677

ISBN-13: 978-1-56383-236-9
ISBN-10: 1-56383-236-4

Item #6222

Table of Contents

Indoor Activities

Family Album

Take your family on a stroll down memory lane. Get out all those old boxes of pictures, baby albums, wedding albums, old certificates and documents and spread them out on the living room floor.

Children love seeing pictures of their parents (and themselves) as babies and hearing stories about their own family and stories of growing up. Let your children ask questions about the photos and old documents and try to answer them as best you can. You can spend hours talking with your children about their family, past and present, by using these photos and documents as a starting point.

Wind Chimes

Wind chimes were probably first created in ancient China where an instrument called a "chime" was used to create music. At that time, a chime was a collection of different sized bells that each rang with a different tone. Chimes were used to decorate the pagodas (Buddhist temple buildings in the form of a tower with several stories) throughout Asia. Soon, Asian people filled their homes with wind chimes. The use of wind chimes spread around the world through the teaching of Feng Shui (the study of people's relationships to the environment in which they live in order to achieve maximum harmony with the spiritual forces believed to influence all places). Wind chimes are believed to have healing powers to enhance the mind, spirit and body of a person.

Your family can create their own wind chimes by hanging different sized washers from a stick or ruler with pieces of string. To make a more colorful chime, paint the washers first with fingernail polish or color them with permanent markers – just make sure to protect the work surface area before using the polish or markers!

Kitchen Gardening

Buy various fruits and vegetables at your local market. Carefully cut the fruits open to reveal the seeds. Remove the seeds from the fruit or vegetable and have your children plant them in small pots or glasses. Place them on your kitchen windowsill so your children can watch the seeds grow into plants, which may bear the fruit again! Some fruits or vegetables that work well in this exercise are:

Avocados

Plant the seed immediately after removing it from the fruit. Carefully slice a very thin layer from both the top and bottom (wider portion) of the seed. Push three toothpicks around the seed and place it over a glass filled with water. Position the seed so that the bottom half is immersed in the water and the top half is out of the water. Over the next several weeks, watch as the roots grow out of the seed and into the water. Like most plants, avocado roots need oxygen. Change the water at least every other week before the water gets dirty and is depleted of oxygen. Avocado plants prefer a lot of bright light.

Cucumbers

Remove four or five seeds from a cucumber and plant them in a medium container or peat pot filled with loose soil that has been mixed with organic matter and plant nutrients. Mound up the dirt over the seeds so that the seeds are about 3″ deep. Water once or twice each week, being careful not to make the soil too wet. Once the leaves have sprouted, place the plant outdoors for a few days before transplanting into the ground where it can grow bigger and bear fruit.

Cherry Tomatoes

Squeeze the seeds out of a cherry tomato and rub them between your fingers to remove the tomato flesh. Set the seeds out to dry on paper towels. Once the seeds are dry, plant 2 or 3 of them in a medium container or peat pot filled with loose soil that has been mixed with organic matter and plant nutrients. Water once or twice each week, being careful not to make the soil too wet. Once the tomato plant is about 3″ tall, place the plant outdoors for a few days before transplanting it the ground where it can grow bigger and bear fruit.

Snowman Pins

You will need tongue depressors, pipe cleaners, white paint, black felt tip pen, orange felt tip pen, pin backing and hot glue.

To make one snowman pin, cut 2″ off of one end of the tongue depressor. Color the 2″ piece completely black with the felt tip pen, forming the top hat. Paint the remaining part of the tongue depressor with the white paint. Draw a face and buttons onto the white piece with the black pen and draw a carrot nose with the orange pen. Glue the black piece onto the white piece using hot glue and decorate the rim with a piece of pipe cleaner. Secure the pipe cleaner into place with the hot glue. Secure the pin back onto the back of the snowman with hot glue.

Winter Beach Party

If the winter blahs are getting you down, bring that fun-in-the-sun summer feeling into your home! Spread beach towels out on the living room floor. Have your family wear their swimsuits and flip flops. Sip on smoothies and feast on nachos or hot dogs. You could even make castles out of clay or playdough. Have your camera ready because you'll want to take pictures of your Winter Beach Party!

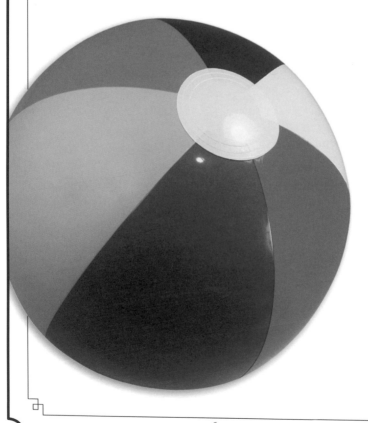

Homemade Snow Globes

You will need jars with lids, small plastic decorative items, oil-based enamel paint, sand paper, super glue, distilled water, glycerin and glitter. Baby food jars are ideal and you can find many small plastic decorative items (such as animals, figures or buildings) in the dollhouse section of your local craft store.

To make one snow globe, paint the jar lid with the enamel paint and set aside to dry. Rub the sand paper over the inside of the jar lid to make a rough surface. Use super glue to adhere the plastic figures to the rough surface of the lid. Fill the jar almost completely with distilled water and drop a pinch of glitter and a few drops of glycerin into the water. The glycerin will keep the glitter from falling too quickly. If you add too much glycerin, the glitter will stick to the bottom of the jar when it's flipped. Screw the lid on tightly. Turn the jar over and then back again to let it snow!

Macaroni Frames

You will need empty cereal boxes, scissors, dried pasta, white glue, a paper punch and yarn. Cut one side from the cereal box and fold it into fourths. Once folded, cut a large rectangle out of the cardboard, cutting at the thickest corner. Unfold the cardboard and you will have a frame. Repeat this with other cereal boxes until there is a cardboard frame for every member of the family.

Have each member decorate their frame with the different shapes of dried pasta, attaching the pasta to the cardboard with the white glue. Use the frames to hold pieces of family art, poems or a favorite card. Punch two holes in either side of the frame and use the yarn to make loops to hang up the Macaroni Frames.

Crayons of
Many Colors

You will need disposable cupcake tins, non-stick cooking spray and broken crayons of many colors.

Spray each disposable cupcake tin with non-stick cooking spray. Preheat the oven to 300°. Remove all the paper from the old crayons and break them into 1″ pieces or smaller. Fill each cupcake tin half full with the different colored crayon pieces. Place the cupcake tin in the oven for about 6 minutes, or until all of the crayons have partially melted into one. Be sure not to let the crayons melt completely because the wax will meld into one grayish color. Remove the tins from the oven and let cool completely. Carefully remove the wax crayon cake from the tin.

To form a rainbow striped crayon cake, melt all crayon pieces of one color at a time. Remove from oven and let that layer cool before adding the next color. Place in oven until layers have melted together. Remove from oven and let harden before adding the next color. Use the crayon cakes to draw or write colorful messages!

Stained-Glass Ornaments

Cut an ornament shape out of heavyweight paper. Use glue to drizzle lines onto the ornament. The glue lines will be the black part of the "stained-glass". Set the ornament aside overnight and let the glue dry completely. After the glue has dried, wrap a piece of aluminum foil, shiny-side-up, completely around the ornament covering both sides. Press down on the aluminum foil so the glue lines are indented through the foil. Use colored markers to color over the aluminum foil, using a different color for each part separated by the glue lines. Punch a hole through the top of the ornament and use a piece of yarn or ribbon to make a loop for hanging on a tree or in the window.

Summer Centerpiece

Thoroughly clean an empty ½ gallon cardboard milk or orange juice carton. Place a candle in the center of the carton and pour water around the candle to within 1″ of the top of the wick. Gather flowers and leaves and tuck them in the water around the candle. Carefully place the carton in the freezer until the water is completely frozen. Before setting the table, remove the carton from the freezer and peel away the cardboard. Set the centerpiece in a tray and light the candle. The tray will catch the water from the melting ice.

Colored Candles

You will need a dull pencil, pillar candles, watercolor brush, acrylic paints, cotton swabs and rubbing alcohol.

Use the dull point of the pencil to etch a design into the wax of the candle. Don't press too hard, but gently go over the lines once or twice with the pencil to create a shallow groove that will catch the paint. Use the watercolor brush and acrylic paints to brush paint color over the grooves. Dilute the paint as you brush by occasionally dipping the brush in water. Let the paint set for about 5 minutes. Wipe away the excess paint with the cotton swabs dipped in rubbing alcohol. The color from the paint will remain only in the etched designs.

Tie Dye

Water
Lemon yellow, fuchsia and
turquoise dye*

Various white cotton
clothing garments
Rubber bands

Fill a few very large pots, buckets or tubs with water and add dye according to package directions. Mix dyes according to the chart below to make desired colors. Wrap rubber bands tightly around white clothing, such as t-shirts, tank tops and shorts. Wherever the rubber bands are placed, there will be a white marking on the clothing. Submerge the clothing pieces in the dyed water, pushing down with long tongs or a stick. Let each clothing piece sit in the dye for at least 15 to 20 minutes. The longer the clothing remains in the dye, the darker the color will become. Remove clothing from the dye and rinse under cool water, according to dye package directions. Ring out garments until water runs clear. Carefully remove rubber bands by using a scissors to cut them from the dye garments. Let dyed garments dry completely.

* You should be able to make a wide array of colors from mixing yellow, fuchsia and turquoise dye. For example,

4 parts fuchsia and 1 part yellow: red

1 part red and 1 part yellow: orange

1 part yellow and 2 parts turquoise: green

4 parts turquoise and 1 part fuchsia: blue

2 parts turquoise and 1 part fuchsia: purple

Family Album Ornaments

Have every member of your family pick out a photo of themselves. Then, fill the work area with creative materials, such as Styrofoam balls, popsicle sticks, scrapbook papers, pipe cleaners, ribbons, yarn, etc.

The idea is that every member of the family will create an ornament using their own photo. The only requirement is that the ornament must reflect the personality of its creator. Make sure that everyone includes the date and year somewhere on the ornament. This activity could be repeated year after year, until you have a tree filled with family faces through time. It will turn into a virtual family album.

Thanksgiving Tree

Draw a big tree on a large piece of poster board and have someone in the family color it in, adding grass, birds, clouds, etc. Create a template of a leaf design out of cardboard and trace the leaf onto many different colored construction papers. Have the other members of the family cut out as many leaves as possible. As soon as the tree is done, attach an empty envelope to the bottom of the poster board to hold a marker, tape and the cut-out leaves. Every time someone in the family is thankful for something, they can write it on one of the leaves and attach their leaf to the tree. Soon the tree will be filled with beautiful, colorful Thanksgiving leaves. This is a great activity to start the week leading up to Thanksgiving.

Puppet Show

Create homemade puppets out of small lunch bags. Decorate the bags with markers, paints, felt, fabric, construction paper, yarn, ribbon, buttons or beads. You will also need scissors and glue to complete this project.

Encourage your family to get creative (or everyone could make a puppet that looks like themselves so you could host a Puppet Family Get-Together). Another idea is to make animal puppets, such as a frog that opens its mouth to catch flies or a snake with a long tongue. Create the face design on the bottom flap of the lunch bag and stick your hand into the bag, using your hand and fingers to control the puppet's "mouth".

Egg Carton Farm

Cut the cups out of egg cartons and turn them over to create little farm or zoo animals. Help everyone get creative by having pictures or photos of real animals around to reference. Also fill the work area with materials like markers, paints, felt, fabric, construction paper, yarn, ribbon, buttons or beads to help everyone create different animals.

Create as many different kinds of animals as you can think of and have fun playing. You could also create fences or pens from the leftover scraps of the egg cartons.

Sand Painting

You will need a pencil, colored chalk, ziplock bags, salt, glue and pieces of cardboard.

Use the pencil to draw a design on the piece of cardboard. Place the different colored pieces of chalk each in a separate ziplock bag. Close the bags securely, letting out any air. Use a hammer or other heavy object to crush the chalk in the bag. Add a little salt to each bag and mix together. Separate the different colored "sand" into small bowls or egg cartons. Spread a thin layer of glue entirely over every area in the drawing that you want to be filled with a certain color. Sprinkle that color over the glue and shake the excess sand back into its container. Let the glue dry slightly before spreading glue over the area to fill with the next color. Continue this pattern until the original drawing is completely filled in with colored sand.

Family Theater

Find a script to a play that is appropriate for all ages. Have each member of the family play one or a few characters in the play. Help create the proper costume from different clothes, jackets, hats or materials around the home. Kids will really love getting to play their part!

Our Family Song

Rewrite the words to a familiar tune, such as Jingle Bells or Mary Had a Little Lamb using your own family lyrics! Have each family member add one line to the song. When you've created a masterpiece, write the lyrics here:

_____

_____

_____

_____

_____

_____

_____

_____

_____

_____

_____

_____

_____

_____

_____

_____

_____

_____

_____

_____

_____

Family Awards Night

This is a fun activity and celebration to honor the special things about each member of the family. Ask everyone to dress up like they are going to a ball or an actual awards night, complete with ties for the gentlemen and dresses or skirts for the ladies. Before getting dressed up, have everyone decorate a piece of paper for the other members of the family, so everyone will be creating one certificate for every member of the family except for themselves. Provide markers and crayons so the awarder can decorate his or her certificates to hand out. Each certificate should include why the awarder thinks that member of the family is special and a valuable person.

Before the awards ceremony begins, serve a fancy meal or decorate the home with balloons or candles. Add an extra touch by playing music softly in the background. During the awards ceremony, each person gets to stand and be recognized as the other family members present their certificates and explain why that person is a special member of the family.

Creative Calendar

You don't have to work for the government in order to create a holiday. Purchase or create a calendar that has plenty of space to write for each day. Let your entire family fill in any day they wish as an "Official Family Holiday". Get creative and have fun celebrating the holidays! Here are a few ideas to get you started:

January 5th: Official Kiss your Pet Day

August: Super Sundae Month (Ice cream sundaes served every Sunday of the month)

October 14th: Eat Dessert First Day

June 6th: Purple and Green Day

Create Your Own Word Scramble

You will need one sheet of paper and a pencil for each player and a stopwatch. Before the game begins, on a sheet of paper, type or write out the words below (or use your own words) to make a master list. Print one copy for yourself. Then retype or rewrite the words with the letters of each word in a scrambled order. Add more words or take words off the list as desired. Print or make copies of the scrambled words so there are enough sheets for each player to have 1 sheet of scrambled words.

When you are ready to begin, give each player a sheet of the scrambled words and 1 pencil. Tell the players to try to unscramble as many of the words on the list as they can within 5 minutes. After 5 minutes, collect all pencils from the players and read the correct unscrambled words from your master list. The player with the most correct answers is the winner.

- Family
- Entertainment
- Fun
- Reunion
- Dinnertime
- Games
- Laughter
- The Family Last Name
- The Name of Each Member of the Family

Family Game Night

Designate one night of the week to play family games together. Play board games, trivia games or card games. This activity is sure to provide an entire evening of laughter and learning that will bring the entire family together. Teach your children how to play games that you played as a child, such as Go Fish, Dominoes, Checkers, Chess or Spoons (directions on the following page). There are also a lot of great board games, educational games and trivia games available in most local stores.

Spoons

You will need one deck of cards without Jokers and spoons. You will need one less spoon that the amount of players, for example: 4 spoons for 5 players, 9 spoons for 10 players, etc. The object of this game is to collect four matching cards (4 aces, 4 sevens, etc.) and to not be the person left without a spoon.

Place the spoons in the middle of the table, making sure they are within grabbing distance of all players. Deal 4 cards to each player and the dealer keeps the deck. The dealer starts the game by picking up 1 card from the deck, deciding if he or she wants to keep it and passing it on. If any player decides to keep the passed card, they must discard 1 card from their hand, making sure to only have 4 cards at a time. The dealer continues passing cards around the circle. Once one player has four of a kind, he or she can grab a spoon from the pile. Once someone has grabbed a spoon from the pile, the rest of the players are free to grab a spoon. The player without a spoon is out of the game. The game continues by eliminating the player without a spoon and 1 spoon from the pile. The cards are reshuffled and dealt. The winner is the last player still alive.

Note: This game is very exciting when the dealer passes the cards as quickly as possible and the player with four of a kind is very discreet when grabbing a spoon. Sometimes players will continue playing for quite a while before realizing there is a missing spoon.

The Memory Game

10 to 15 small items
1 serving tray
1 cloth, big enough to cover the tray
1 piece of paper and pencil for each player

Place the 10 to 15 small items on a serving tray. Use items such as a pencil, watch, comb, shoelace, spoon or toy car. Cover the tray with a cloth. Have all the family members sit in a circle. Place the tray in the middle of the circle and remove the cloth for 30 to 60 seconds. Tell everyone to look at the tray. When the time is up, remove the tray or replace the cloth over the tray. Hand one piece of paper and a pencil or pen to each family member and give them 60 seconds to write down as many of the items as they can remember. The player who remembered the most correct items wins.

Variation: Instead of writing down the items, have each player name one item from the tray. The player next to them has to name a different item and so on. The first person to fail to name an item, repeat an item or name something not on the tray is out. Then the tray is removed, replaced with some or all new items and returned for the next round. The game restarts with all players except those who are out. If the game is too easy for the group, add more items or reduce the time.

Family Trivia

Use different colored index cards for each member of the family. For example, the pink cards are used for Mom, the green cards are used for Dad, etc. Write down questions about each family member on their colored card with the answers also written on the same side of each card. Write questions that only family members would know the answer to, such as, "Mom really wanted to go on vacation here last summer," or "How did Bobby lose his front tooth?" The game can be played individually, as teams, using a game board or just as a trivia contest. This is also a great activity to help learn more about each member of the family.

You can also incorporate photos, video taped events or tape recordings to tie in with the questions, for example, show a clip from a family reunion and push pause. The question could be, "Name as many people on screen as possible" or "When was this family reunion held?" or "Who won the egg toss at this family reunion?"

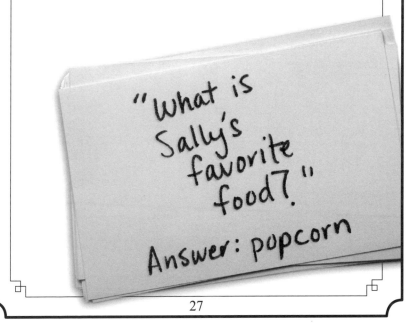

"What is Sally's favorite food?"

Answer: popcorn

The Question Game

You will need one chair for each player. This game is best if played with 4 or more players. Arrange the chairs in a circle. Have each player sit in one chair. The first player starts by asking someone else in the circle a question. That person has to then ask another person in the circle a question, and so on. Any player who answers the questions, laughs or stares in confusion is out. Some good questions to ask are, "Huh?", "Are we playing yet?" and "Why are you wearing a hat?"

The Silly Hat and Gloves Game

You will need one serving tray, one silly hat, one scarf, one pair of big gloves, one butter knife, one fork, one piece of chocolate that is tightly wrapped and one pair of dice. Have all the family members sit in a circle and place the tray in the middle of the circle. On the tray, place the silly hat, scarf, gloves, knife, fork and wrapped bar of chocolate. Have the players take turns rolling one of the die. If the player rolls a 1, 2, 3, 4 or 5, their turn is over and the next player to the right throws the die. However, if the player throws a 6, that player must immediately put on the hat, scarf and gloves. After this, the player must immediately start trying to unwrap the chocolate, using only the knife and fork. The other players continue rolling the die as quickly as they can. If another player rolls a 6 while the first player is trying to open the candy, the first player immediately stops what they are doing and the new player puts on the hat, scarf and gloves and tries to open the chocolate. The winner is the first player to successfully open the chocolate and eat it before any other players roll a 6.

King's Corners

You will need one deck of cards and at least two or more players. The object of the game is to be the first person to get rid of all your cards. Determine which player is the dealer. Have the dealer deal seven cards to each player. Place the rest of the cards face-down in the center of the table. The dealer then turns over the four top cards, lying one card face-up spreading from each side of the deck. Each player must pick up one card from the center pile at the beginning of each turn. The first player to the left has a turn to try to get rid of some of their cards by laying them on the face-up piles. If a player has a King, the King can be placed face-up at a diagonal (in the corners) from the center pile. A card can be laid on the face-up piles if it is in descending order and the opposite color of the face-up card. For example, only a red Queen can be laid on a black King, only a red 6 can be placed on a black 7, only a black Ace can be set on a red 2. An entire line of descending cards can be moved to another line if the first (the bottom card) in the pile would be correctly placed in order on another line. When an entire line is moved, creating an open space, that player can place any card from his or her hand in that space. A player can continue their turn as long as he or she has cards to lie down. The first player to lay down all of their cards is the winner.

Outdoor Activities

Family Car Wash

Get the entire family involved the next time you wash the car(s). Make sure everyone dresses in the swimsuits or old clothes that they won't mind getting wet. Gather lots of buckets filled with soapy water and hoses so everyone can join in the fun. The water fights will be inevitable, so just let them happen and join in! It may be a good idea to clean the trash out of the car and vacuum the inside before or after the water fights. When the car is cleaned, reward everyone with a trip to the swimming pool or an ice cream cone!

A Walk With A Twist

A family walk around the neighborhood doesn't have to be boring. The next time you all gather for a stroll, take a quarter with you. Begin the walk by throwing the quarter up in the air. If it lands on tails, your walk begins by turning left. If it lands on heads, your walk begins by turning right. Continue to do this at every corner, letting everyone take turns tossing the quarter up in the air and reading the outcome.

Snowball Target

When the ground is covered in snow, turn the next snowball fight into a throwing contest. You will need spray bottles, food coloring and sticks with flags. Stomp out a huge circle in the snow. This will be your target. Then, fill the spray bottles with water and a few drops of food coloring in each. Spray the colored water onto the snow in smaller rings inside the target. Mark each section with a flag and write the number of points that section is worth. Have the sections be worth more the closer they are to the very center of the circle. To play the game, everyone will need to assemble their own snowballs and throw them into the target from a designated point. Keep track of how many points each family member gets. The first person to reach 100 points is the winner.

Clothesline Theater

Create your own outdoor theater by hanging large sheets from a clothesline for the backdrop. Use an old sheet, so the family can paint a scene on the sheet, or cut out scenery from construction paper and pin it to the backdrop. Hang two other sheets from a clothesline suspended six feet in front of the backdrop. Use 1¼″ binder clips to hang the front sheets. The clothesline should go through the triangular center of the binder clips so the actors can slide the curtains open and closed.

Snow Painting

If you want to get outdoors in the winter, why not encourage your family to do some Snow Painting. Fill several spray bottles with water and a few drops of a different colored food coloring in each. These will act as the paint. Lead the family out to the yard or a wide open field and explain that the snow is the canvas and everyone can use their paint to fill it with colorful drawings and designs. It is also fun to assemble a snowman together and to paint his clothes on with the spray bottles.

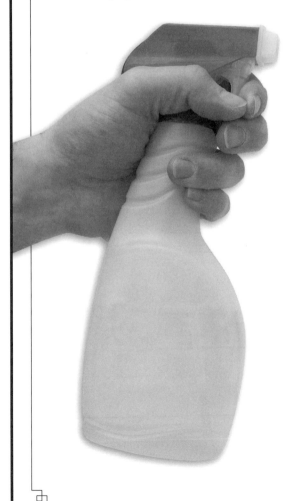

Lion's Cub

You will need at least five players and one football. Choose one player to be the first "lion". Designate something in the area to be "base" (a lawn chair, a tree, the porch, etc.). The lion sits on the ground with the football placed right behind his or her back. The remaining players try to sneak up behind the player and steal the football (the cub) and take it back to base before they are caught by the lion. When the lion suspects there is someone trying to steal his or her cub, the lion turns around and roars at the player and immediately starts chasing him or her back to base. If the lion catches the player before that player reaches base, that player is out of the game. If a player can grab the football and return to base before the lion catches him or her, then the lion is out of the game and a new lion is chosen. If the lion mistakenly turns around and roars when there are no players trying to steal his or her cub, then the lion is out of the game and a new lion is chosen. The last player remaining in the game is the winner.

Song Tag

Play this game just like regular tag, designating one person to be "it". That person chases everyone around the yard. All the other players can save themselves just as they are about to be caught by sitting on the ground and starting to sing a favorite song. If everyone sits down at once, at least one person has to get back on their feet and start running or else everyone is out. A person is also out if they start to sing a song that they've already sung. You could substitute songs by having everyone name something else just as they are about to be tagged, such as a food, television show or state. Remember, someone who yells out a repeat answer or song is fair game for being tagged.

Outdoor Scavenger Hunt

Make a list for each family member of ten things that are found outdoors, such as feathers, leaves, acorns, flowers, etc. Give a copy of the list to each player and send them out to collect the items. The first one back to the house with all items (or the most items) on the list within 10 minutes is the winner. You can make the scavenger hunt as easy or as difficult as you like by listing items that are easy or difficult to find.

Balloon Relay

You will need 10 to 20 balloons filled with air and two baskets. Divide everyone into two even teams and have each team stand in a line. Give each team half of the balloons in a basket. The first in each line takes a balloon from the basket and runs, as fast as they can, to the other side of the yard and sits or stomps on the balloon to pop it. After popping the balloon they return to the line and tag the next person. The next person does the same thing and so on. The winning team is the first to pop all of their balloons.

Mother Nature Games

You don't need fancy equipment and accessories to have fun outdoors. Encourage your family to get crafty by creating daisy or dandelion chains from all those flowers growing outdoors. Just be careful not to pick from your neighbors plantings! Tie the stems of the flowers together to create a long chain or flower jewelry. Flowers with stiff stems work the best.

You can also teach your family how to make a whistle from a simple piece of grass. Pull one blade of long, flat grass from the ground. Place the blade of grass between both of your thumbs, holding it tightly together at the top and bottom. The natural curve of your thumbs should leave a small opening in the middle between the blade of grass and your thumbs. Put your lips up to your thumbs and blow hard. This should make a whistling sound. Crabgrass works best and different kinds of grass make different sounds.

Sprinkler Freeze Tag

Use a long hose to connect a sprinkler from the water source out to an open area. Designate one person to control the water source, turning the water on and off. Preferably, this person should be out of sight of everyone else.

Have the rest of the family dance around the sprinkler, making funny faces and being silly. The person controlling the sprinkler can choose when to turn it on randomly. As soon as the water comes out of the sprinkler, everyone else has to freeze in the position they are in until the sprinkler turns off again. This activity is sure to bring lots of laughter!

Blind Man Ball Game

You will need at least six players for this game, two big baskets, six balls of any size and two handkerchiefs.

Separate the players into two even teams. Each team will have one basket filled with three balls and one handkerchief. Place the baskets of balls six feet in front of each team. Blindfold the first player of each team with the handkerchiefs and dump the balls from the basket. The blindfolded players will have to retrieve the three balls, one at a time, and return them to their team's basket before passing the handkerchief to the next player. The non-blindfolded players can help their blindfolded teammate by giving verbal directions only. The blindfolded player can retrieve any of the balls (even the ones from the other team) but they must be returned to their team's basket. If he or she puts the ball(s) in the wrong basket, they will count for the other team. Once the blindfolded player has put three balls in their team's basket, the next player is blindfolded and the balls are dumped from the basket. The winning team is the first to complete one rotation of players.

Pass the Sand

You will need two buckets half filled with sand, two paper plates and one food scale. This game should be played outdoors and is best when played with a lot of people. Divide the players into two even teams. Have each team stand in a line. Pour one bucket of sand into the hands of the first player on each team. Have the players pass the sand in their hands to the next player and so on until the sand has reached the end of the line. Have the last player dump the sand in their hands onto a paper plate. Compare the amounts of sand on the two paper plates by placing them on the food scale. The team that has passed the most amount of sand down the line wins the game.

Four Square

Use chalk to draw a ten-foot square on the pavement or driveway. Then, divide the big square into 4 even squares. Number the squares one through four, going clockwise. Draw a diagonal line in box number one to be the serving line. Place one player in each of the boxes. The person in box one serves the ball from behind the diagonal line by bouncing it into any of the other boxes and trying to prevent it from being bounced back into their own square. If the player returns the ball to square one, then the server is out and everyone moves up one square. If the player doesn't return the ball (by hitting it out of bounds, or if the ball bounces off the player and out of bounds without hitting the ground first), then that player is out and everyone moves up one square and a new player enters box four. The object of the game is to always hit the ball into another person's square after it bounces in your box and, eventually, to move up to box one and to stay there.

Chain Hide n' Seek

Chain Hide n' Seek is played just like regular hide n' seek, but with a twist. One person is designated to be "it". That person closes their eyes and counts to 50 while everyone else runs to a hiding spot. Once the person designated to be "it" finds someone, they get to take that person by the hand and together they search for everyone else. The chain continues to grow as they keep adding people as they are found.

Another variation to the regular hide n' seek, is called Sardines. When playing Sardines, one person is designated to be "it". Everyone else closes their eyes and counts to 50 while "it" runs to a hiding spot. Everyone else scatters trying to find "it". Once a player finds where "it" is hiding, they have to quietly sit down and join "it" in the hiding spot while the rest of the group tries to find them. The hiding spot continues to grow as more and more people find the hiding spot.

500

You will need three or more players and one football. Designate one player as the first "thrower". Have all players except for the thrower stand in a cluster that is within throwing distance away from the thrower. The thrower holds the football and yells out a number between 50 and 500 and throws the football at the cluster of players. If one of the players catches the ball, he or she would receive the number of points that the thrower yelled out. However, if he or she drops the ball, they would lose that number of points (negative points are possible). The thrower continues to throw the ball and call out numbers. The first person to rack up 500 or more points becomes the new thrower.

Make Your Own Bean Bag Toss

Circular saw
1 (4′ x 8′) piece
   of ½″ plywood
1 (7′) piece of 1″ x 1″ board
Yardstick
Pencil

Reciprocating saw or jigsaw
Wood glue
C-clamps
Drill
1″ wood screws
Paint

Using the circular saw, cut the 4′ x 8′ piece of plywood in half to make two 4′ x 4′ pieces.* Set one of the 4′ x 4′ pieces aside. Using the pencil, divide the remaining piece of 4′ x 4′ plywood in half diagonally and saw this piece in half using the circular saw. You should now have two diagonally-cut pieces of plywood. Mark the midpoint of the 7 foot board and cut on that line to make two pieces of 3½′ board (Diagram 1). Mark 1, 2 or 3 holes on the front of the remaining 4′ x 4′ board. These holes will act as the beanbag holes. Each hole should be approximately 5″ to 6″ in diameter. Cut

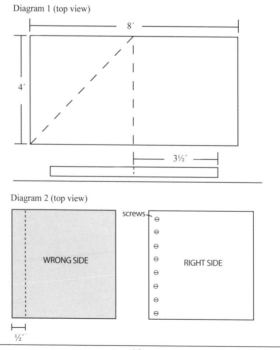

Diagram 1 (top view)

8′

4′

3½′

Diagram 2 (top view)

screws

WRONG SIDE

RIGHT SIDE

½′

out the holes with a reciprocating saw or jigsaw. Down both sides of the board, draw a line with the pencil that is ½″ in from either edge. Turn the game board over on a flat surface and, with the pencil, mark the appropriate sides of the board with "top" and "bottom". Place one of the 3½′ boards along one side of the game board (not the top or the bottom), ½″ in from the edge. Use wood glue to hold the plywood and the board together. Attach C-clamps to hold the board in place and turn the board over so the right side is up. Drill screws along the line marked ½″ in on either side of the board. Drill 1 screw approximately every inch (Diagram 2). Turn the board over again and place the remaining 3½′ board on the other side of the plywood piece, glue, clamp and turn over again to drill board in place. Turn the board face down again and place one diagonal piece along the inside of each 3½′ board, so that the long piece of the diagonal boards would sit flat on the ground when the bean bag toss is upright. Glue and clamp boards in place, turn over and place a screw every 1″ so diagonal boards are attached (Diagram 3). Reinforce the boards by drilling screws through the sides of the 3½′ boards and into the diagonal pieces. Sit the bean bag toss upright so the front of the board rests at an angle and paint the face of the board as desired (Diagram 4).

*Note: Many home improvement stores and lumber stores will cut your plywood for you at little or no charge.

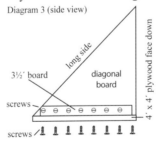

Diagram 3 (side view)

Diagram 4 (angled view)

Bagg-O

You will need two Bean Bag Toss Boards, two bean bags and at least two players. Place the two bean bag toss boards approximately 20′ apart on the ground facing each other. To make your own Bean Bag Toss, see directions on page 48. Divide all players into two teams and have each team stand next to one of the bean bag boards. The two teams take turns tossing the bean bags at the other team's board. Each team gets 3 tosses per turn. The scoring is as follows:

- A bean bag that goes through a hole is worth 2 points.
- A bean bag that lands on the board but does not go all the way through the hole (even if it rests partially in the hole) is worth 1 point.
- The first team to reach 21 points is the winning team.
- A team can cancel out the opposing team's points by gaining the same amount of points on the following turn. For example, if Team A got 6 points during one round and Team B got 6 points on their very next turn, Team A would not receive 6 points. However, Team A would now have a chance to cancel out Team B's 6 points by earning 6 points on their next turn.

Frisbee Bocce Ball

You will need at least two players, a large open space and one Frisbee for each player. Divide the players into two even teams. Have one player choose an object somewhere within the playing space (a tree, a lawn chair, a rock, etc.). Each player takes turns trying to throw their Frisbee near the chosen object. The three players who land their Frisbee closest to the object gain points for his or her team. The rules and scoring are as follows:

- The player with the Frisbee closest to the object gets 3 points.

- The player with the second closest Frisbee gets 2 points.

- The player with the third closest Frisbee gets 1 point.

- A player can knock another player's Frisbee farther away from the object.

- The first team to score 15 points wins.

- After each round of play, have another player pick a new object at which to throw the Frisbees.

Peg in a Bottle

You will need one long piece of string, one pencil, one empty 2-litre bottle and at least two players. Tie one end of the string securely around the pencil. Tie the other end of the string around the waist of a player so the pencil hangs down in front of the player. Set the empty bottle on the ground in the middle of the playing area.

Each player gets a chance to try to lower the pencil into the empty bottle by squatting over the bottle. However, the player can not use his or her hands to try to lower the "peg" into the bottle. The remaining players count out loud to 10. If the player can lower the peg into the bottle before the remaining players count to 10, then it is another player's turn to tie the string around his or her waist and lower the peg. However, if the player cannot lower the peg into the bottle before the remaining players count to 10, then that player is eliminated. Play continues until all but one player has been eliminated.

Down, Down, Down

You will need at least two players and one Frisbee. Have all players stand apart but within throwing distance of each other.

Toss the Frisbee back and forth until one of the players drops the Frisbee (it has to be a catch-able toss). Any player who drops the Frisbee has to play with 1 knee on the ground and the tossing continues. If a player drops the Frisbee again, he or she has to play with both knees on the ground. If a player drops the Frisbee for a third time, he or she has to play with 1 elbow on the ground and the tossing continues. If a player drops the Frisbee for a fourth time, he or she has to put both knees and both elbows on the ground and he or she is out. The last player remaining without all knees and elbows on the ground is the winner!

Backyard Volcano

You will need a 9 x 13″ baking dish, a 20-ounce soda bottle, moist soil, 1 tablespoon baking soda, 1 cup vinegar and red food coloring.

Place the baking dish on the grass and set the soda bottle in the middle of the baking dish. Mound the soil up around the bottle to form the mountain. Pack the dirt right up to the bottle opening, but be careful not to get any soil inside of the bottle. Pour the baking soda into the bottle. In a glass measuring cup, combine the vinegar and a few drops of food coloring. Pour the vinegar into the bottle over the baking soda and stand back as the volcano erupts!

Homemade Kites

You will need two sheets of newspaper, construction paper, kite string, fabric scraps, glue, tape, markers and a light breeze!

To make one kite, fold one of the newspaper sheets in half and roll it up tightly to make a pole. Tape it closed at both ends and in the middle. Do the same with the other piece of newspaper. Make a cross with the two newspaper poles and tie them together in the middle. Tie the string to one end of the one of the poles and then wrap it around the end of the pole next to it. Continue doing this, securing the string with tape, until the string forms four diagonal lines and the frame of the kite. Lay the kite frame over a large piece of construction paper and trace the edges. Cut a line that is about 1″ larger than this shape on all sides. Cut off each of the four pointed corners. Use crayons, markers, additional construction paper and glue to decorate the cut out shape. Lay the kite frame on the back of the cut-out kite and fold the extra 1″ of paper over the string on one side. Secure it tightly with tape and repeat with the remaining three sides. Add a tail to your kite made out of string and fabric scraps and tie a long piece of string from the middle of the kite. Your kite is finished and you can go test it out in the light breeze.

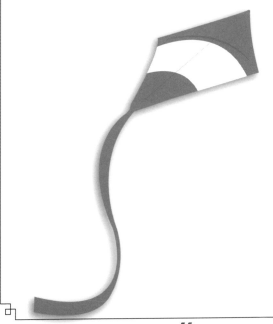

Milk Jug
Bird Feeders

Rinse out an empty gallon milk jug that has a lid. Hold the jug upside down and cut the handle part out of the jug. Cut two small holes in the plastic and insert pencils in the holes for the birds to perch on. Attach a piece of wire to hang the jug to a branch or bird feeder stand. Fill the bottom of the jug with birdseed and hang the feeder outdoors. Sit quietly and wait for the birds to come enjoy their treat!

Capture Sounds

The next time you go out for a family walk, hike or picnic, take a small tape recorder with you. Instead of taking pictures to record the memories, use the tape recorder to record the sounds of birds singing, flowing water, swings squeaking, crunching leaves, wind blowing and children playing. Tape each sound separately and then play the tape on the drive or walk home and see if the family can identify each sound. You may want to wait a few days or weeks before playing the tape, as this will help spark memories and can turn into a fun game trying to remember what thing or person generated each sound.

Flying Babies

You will need one soft "cushy" ball and at least three players. Designate one player as the first "thrower". Give all remaining players a different number. All remaining players cluster around the thrower. The thrower tosses the ball up in the air and yells, "Baby in the air" followed by a number of one of the players. The player whose number is called has to catch the ball while all remaining players (including the thrower) scatter in all directions.

As soon as the player catches the ball, he or she has to yell, "Freeze!" All remaining players have to freeze where they are. Then the player with the ball can take three steps in any direction. The player then tries to throw the ball at any of the other players. If the player hits another player, the hit player gets a "B". If the player throwing the ball misses another player, the throwing player gets a "B". The process goes again until one player has enough letters to spell "BABY". When any player has four letters, they are out. The last person remaining is the winner!

Washer Toss

You will need at least two players, two empty coffee cans, two large cardboard boxes, four metal washers and paint.

Divide the players into two even teams. Paint the washers in two different colors so there are two washers of each color. Set the two cardboard boxes approximately 15′ apart on the ground. Set one empty coffee can inside each cardboard box. Each team can place the coffee can any place within their cardboard box. Have each team stand next to one of the cardboard boxes. The two teams take turns tossing the washers at the other team's box. Each team gets 2 tosses per turn. The scoring is as follows:

- A washer that lands outside of the box is worth 0 points.

- A washer that lands in the cardboard box is worth 1 point.

- A washer that lands in the empty coffee can is worth 2 points.

- The first team to reach 21 points is the winning team. The team must reach exactly (not over) 21 points to win the game.

Crazy Olympics

Invent your own Crazy Olympics in your backyard by creating events such as the Backwards Crab Walk, Blindfolded Leapfrog, Frisbee Golf, Impossible Obstacle Course, etc. Add relay races such as pass the eggs, three-legged races or carry a cotton ball on a spoon. Be sure to create silly medals to award the winners of each competition.

Family
Snacks

Watermelon Granita

Makes 6 servings

1 (4 lb.) watermelon
⅓ C. sugar
⅓ C. water

2 T. fresh lime juice
6 thin watermelon wedges

Remove the seeds from the watermelon and cut the watermelon fruit into 1″ cubes. In a small saucepan, combine sugar and water. Bring to a boil over high heat, stirring until the sugar is completely dissolved. Transfer the sugar mixture to a blender or food processor. Add half of the watermelon cubes. Add lime juice and pulse until smooth. Add remaining watermelon cubes and blend until smooth. Pour the watermelon puree through a large-holed strainer, pressing down on the solids. Transfer mixture to a 9 x 13″ baking dish and place in freezer. Stir every 30 minutes with a fork, until all the liquid has frozen completely, about 3 hours. To serve, spoon the Watermelon Granita into tall glasses or bowls. Garnish with watermelon wedges. Freeze up to 2 days. Stir before serving.

Old Fashioned Pink Lemonade

Makes about 3 cups

2 C. water
½ C. sugar
¼ C. fresh squeezed
  lemon juice

2 tsp. grenadine or
  cherry juice

    In a pitcher, combine water, sugar, lemon juice and grenadine, mixing until the sugar is completely dissolved. Divide lemonade into glasses filled with ice cubes. This lemonade can also be frozen into popsicle mold or mixed with other fruit juices for a fun combination, such as orange juice, pineapple juice or white grape juice.

Orange Glorious

Makes 4 servings

1 (6 oz.) can frozen orange juice concentrate
¾ C. milk

¼ C. water
1 tsp. vanilla
12 ice cubes

In a blender, combine frozen orange juice concentrate, milk, water and vanilla. Process on high until blended and smooth. Add ice cubes and blend until ice is evenly crushed. Pour orange mixture into glasses and serve.

Raspberry Banana Chocolate Smoothies

Makes 4 servings

1½ C. chocolate milk
1½ C. chocolate ice cream
2½ C. frozen unsweetened
   raspberries

1 banana, peeled and sliced
1 to 2 fresh chopped mint
   leaves, optional

In a blender, combine chocolate milk, chocolate ice cream, raspberries and sliced banana. Blend until smooth. Pour blended mixture into four tall glasses. If desired, garnish with chopped mint leaves.

Chocolate
Mint Milkshakes

Makes 4 servings

8 scoops vanilla ice cream
½ C. milk

½ C. chocolate syrup
4 drops peppermint extract

In a blender, combine vanilla ice cream, milk, chocolate syrup and peppermint extract. Blend until smooth. Pour blended mixture into four tall glasses and serve.

Roasted Pumpkin Seeds

Makes 4 cups

4¼ C. raw pumpkin seeds   **1 tsp. coarse salt**
1 T. vegetable oil

After the fall harvest and pumpkin carving are complete, collect the pumpkin seeds to make this tasty (and healthy) family snack!

Thoroughly clean the pumpkin seeds after removing them from the pumpkin. Remove as much pumpkin pulp from the seeds as possible. In a large bowl, combine cleaned pumpkin seeds, vegetable oil and coarse salt. Toss all together until salt is evenly distributed. Place a sheet of parchment paper over an 11 x 15″ baking sheet. Spread the seed mixture evenly over baking sheet and set aside for 24 to 48 hours, or until seeds have dried, stirring occasionally. Preheat oven to 325° and remove waxed paper from baking sheet. Toast seeds in oven for 35 to 40 minutes, stirring once. Remove from oven and set aside to cool. Pat seeds with paper towels to remove excess oil.

Delicious
Veggie Dip

Makes about 1½ cups

1 C. cottage cheese
½ C. shredded
   Cheddar cheese
1 tsp. dried dillweed

2 tsp. Worcestershire sauce
1 tsp. salt
Fresh cut raw vegetables

In a small bowl, combine cottage cheese, shredded Cheddar cheese, dried dillweed, Worcestershire sauce and salt. Mix until well combined and serve with fresh cut raw vegetables, such as carrots, red pepper slices, celery and cucumbers for dipping.

Homemade Pretzels

Makes about 20 small pretzels

1 (¾ oz.) pkg. active dry yeast	1½ tsp. sugar
1½ C. lukewarm water	4 C. flour
¾ tsp. salt	1 egg
	Coarse salt, optional

Preheat oven to 425°. In a medium bowl, soften the yeast in the lukewarm water. Let set for about 2 minutes and stir in the salt and sugar. Gradually mix in the flour, kneading the dough until it is soft and smooth. Divide the dough into small pieces for every member of the family. Encourage everyone to roll their dough into letters, animal shapes or any design they choose. Just make sure that each pretzel is about the same thickness in all places. Transfer the pretzel creations to a greased baking sheet. In a small bowl, whisk the egg. Brush the egg over each pretzel and, if desired, sprinkle the coarse salt over each pretzel. Bake in oven for about 15 minutes, or until the pretzels are golden brown.

Super Nachos

Makes 6 servings

1 lb. ground beef
1 onion, finely diced
Salt and pepper to taste
1 (14½ oz.) pkg. tortilla chips
1 (16 oz.) can refried beans

2 C. shredded
  Cheddar cheese
1 jalapeno pepper,
  sliced, optional

In a large skillet over medium high heat, cook ground beef and diced onion, stirring often, until beef is browned and onions are softened. Drain fat from skillet and season meat mixture with salt and pepper to taste. To assemble nachos, arrange tortilla chips on a large serving platter. Place dollops of refried beans over chips. Layer half of the shredded Cheddar cheese and half of the ground beef mixture over the beans. Repeat layers with more chips, more refried beans, remaining cheese and remaining beef mixture. If desired, top with slices of jalapeno pepper.

Mini Pizza Snackers

Makes 24 snacks

24 whole wheat crackers
6 American cheese singles, quartered

2 to 4 T. pizza sauce
24 thin pepperoni slices

Preheat oven to 350°. Place whole wheat crackers in a single layer on a baking sheet. Place 1 quartered cheese slice on each cracker and top with ¼ teaspoon to ½ teaspoon pizza sauce. Place 1 pepperoni slice over pizza sauce on each cracker. Bake in oven for 3 to 5 minutes, until cheese is melted. Serve immediately.

Fresh Veggie Squares

Makes 12 servings

1 (8 oz.) pkg. refrigerated
    crescent rolls
1 (8 oz.) pkg. cream cheese,
    softened
¾ C. grated Parmesan cheese
3 T. ranch dressing
½ tsp. hot pepper sauce

1 C. halved cherry tomatoes
1 C. chopped red, yellow or
    green peppers
1 C. chopped broccoli florets
½ C. shredded carrots
Salt to taste

Preheat oven to 375°. Unroll crescent rolls on a lightly greased baking sheet. Pinch dough together to make one 9 x 12″ square of dough. Pinch ¼″ of dough around edges to make a rim in dough. Bake in oven for 12 to 14 minutes, until golden brown. Remove crust from oven and let cool on a wire rack. In a medium bowl, combine cream cheese, grated Parmesan cheese, ranch dressing and hot sauce. Mix well and spread over cooled crust. Over topping on crust, place one row of each chopped vegetable. Press down lightly on tomatoes, peppers, broccoli and carrots. If desired, sprinkle salt over veggies. Cut into 3″ squares and serve immediately or chill in refrigerator, covered, for up to 3 days.

Crispy Cheddar Rounds

Makes 4 dozen

3 slices bacon
½ C. butter, softened
1½ C. shredded
   Cheddar cheese
3 T. water

1 tsp. Worcestershire sauce
⅛ tsp. salt
¾ C. flour
¾ C. quick oats
Grated Parmesan cheese

In a small skillet over medium high heat, cook bacon until browned and crispy. Remove bacon to paper towels to drain. Crumble drained bacon into small pieces. In a medium bowl, combine butter, shredded Cheddar cheese, water, Worcestershire sauce and salt. Stir until well mixed and add flour, oats and crumbled bacon. Mix well and shape mixture into a 12″ log. Cover log with plastic wrap and refrigerate for 4 hours. Preheat oven to 400°. Using a sharp knife, cut roll into ¼″ thick slices. Place rounds face-down, 1″ apart on an ungreased baking sheet. Sprinkle top of each round lightly with grated Parmesan cheese. Bake in oven for 8 to 10 minutes, until lightly browned. Remove from oven and transfer immediately to wire racks to cool. Rounds are best when served warm.

Fruit Pizza

Makes 1 pizza

1 (18 oz.) pkg. refrigerated
    sugar cookie dough
1 (7 oz.) jar
    marshmallow cream

1 (8 oz.) pkg. cream cheese,
    softened
Various fruits, peeled
    and sliced

Preheat oven to 350°. On an ungreased baking sheet, smooth the refrigerated sugar cookie dough into a single layer approximately ¼″ thick. Bake in preheated oven for 10 minutes, until edges are lightly browned and center is no longer doughy. In a medium bowl, blend marshmallow cream with cream cheese. Spread the mixture over the baked crust. Chill in refrigerator until serving. Before serving, decorate pizza with fresh slices of various fruits, such as kiwi, grapes and mangos.

Pink
Raspberry Dip

Makes 24 servings

1 C. sour cream
1 (8 oz.) pkg. Neufchatel
   cheese, softened

½ C. sugar
1 T. raspberry extract
½ C. fresh raspberries

In a medium mixing bowl, beat sour cream, Neufchatel cheese, sugar and raspberry extract at medium speed. Blend until smooth. Chill in the refrigerator for approximately 30 minutes. Garnish with fresh raspberries. Serve as a dip for fresh fruit.

Mini Ham & Cheese Rolls

Makes 24 rolls

2 T. dried minced onion
1 T. prepared mustard
2 T. poppy seeds
½ C. butter, melted

24 dinner rolls
½ lb. ham, chopped
½ lb. Swiss cheese,
 thinly sliced

Preheat oven to 325°. In a small mixing bowl, combine minced onion, mustard, poppy seeds and melted butter. Split each dinner roll. Insert chopped ham and 1 slice Swiss cheese into each roll. Drizzle the poppy seed mixture over the rolls. Bake for 20 minutes, until cheese has melted. Serve warm.

Summer Pickle Roll-Ups

Makes 5 servings

5 slices cooked ham   **5 dill pickle spears**
1 (8 oz.) pkg. cream cheese,
  softened

Lay ham slices on a flat serving plate and pat dry. Spread softened cream cheese over ham. Place 1 dill pickle spear at 1 end of each slice. Roll the ham over the pickle to form a cylinder. Repeat with other ham slices and pickles. Secure ham with a toothpick. If desired, cut slices to make smaller appetizers.

Seven Layered Taco Dip

Makes about 12 servings

1 (1 oz.) pkg. taco seasoning
1 (16 oz.) can refried beans
1 (16 oz.) pkg. sour cream
1 (8 oz.) pkg. cream cheese, softened
1 (16 oz.) jar salsa, any kind
1 large tomato, chopped
1 green bell pepper, chopped

1 bunch green onions, chopped
1 small head iceberg lettuce, shredded
2 C. shredded Cheddar cheese
1 (6 oz.) can black olives, drained and sliced

In a medium bowl, blend taco seasoning and refried beans. Spread mixture evenly onto a large serving platter. Mix the sour cream and cream cheese in a medium bowl. Spread over refried beans. Top with salsa. Place a layer of chopped tomato, green bell pepper, green onions and lettuce over the salsa. Top with Cheddar cheese and garnish with black olives. Serve with chips or veggies for dipping.

Cheeseburger Pizzas

Makes 8 individual pizzas

½ lb. ground beef
½ C. diced pepperoni
1¼ C. pizza sauce
1 C. crumbled feta cheese
½ tsp. Worcestershire sauce
½ tsp. hot pepper sauce

Salt and pepper, to taste
1 (10 oz.) can refrigerated
  biscuit dough
1 egg yolk
1 C. shredded
  mozzarella cheese

Preheat oven to 375°. In a large skillet over medium heat, brown ground beef and drain. Stir in diced pepperoni, pizza sauce and crumbled feta cheese. Add Worcestershire sauce, hot pepper sauce, salt and pepper. Cook for 1 minute, stirring constantly. Grease a large baking sheet. Separate biscuits and place 3″ apart on the prepared baking sheet. Press each biscuit with the bottom of a glass, forming a ½″ ridge around the outside edge of each biscuit. In a small bowl, beat egg yolk with ¼ teaspoon water. Brush egg mixture over sides and edges of biscuits. Spoon ¼ cup beef mixture into each biscuit. Top with sprinkled mozzarella cheese. Bake in oven for 15 to 20 minutes, or until golden brown and cheese bubbles. Let cool for 2 minutes before serving.

Fruit Salsa with Cinnamon Chips

Makes 10 servings

2 kiwis, peeled and diced

2 apples, peeled, cored and diced

8 oz. raspberries

1 lb. sliced strawberries

2 T. sugar

1 T. brown sugar

3 T. fruit preserves, any flavor

10 (10″) flour tortillas

Butter or margarine, softened

1¾ C. sugar

1 T. cinnamon

In a large bowl, combine diced kiwis, diced apples, raspberries, sliced strawberries, sugar, brown sugar and fruit preserves. Cover and chill in refrigerator at least 15 minutes. Preheat oven to 350°. Coat one side of each flour tortilla with a thin layer of the softened butter. Cut into wedges and arrange in a single layer on a large baking sheet. In a small bowl, combine sugar and cinnamon. Sprinkle wedges with cinnamon and sugar mixture. Bake in preheated oven for 8 to 10 minutes. Remove chips from oven and let cool for 15 minutes. Serve with fruit salsa for dipping.

Ocean Gelatin Snacks

Makes 4 servings

1 C. boiling water
1 (3 oz.) pkg. blue gelatin,
  any flavor
1 C. cold water

2 (1 oz.) pkgs. fish-shaped
  fruit snacks
Thawed whipped topping

In a medium bowl, combine boiling water and blue gelatin, mixing until completely dissolved. Stir in cold water. Pour gelatin into 4 tall dessert or parfait glasses, filling about half full. Refrigerate filled glasses for about 1 hour, or until just slightly firm. Press a few fish-shaped fruit snacks into each cup and return to refrigerator for an additional 3 hours. To serve, spread a little whipped topping over gelatin in each cup to look like waves.

Cookie Art

Makes 24 servings

1 (18 oz.) pkg. refrigerated sugar cookie dough	½ tsp. water
Flour	Food coloring
2 egg yolks	Small candies or miniature chocolate chips

Preheat oven 350°. Place the sugar cookie dough crosswise in the middle of a greased 11 x 15″ jellyroll pan. Let stand for about 5 minutes to let the dough soften. Sprinkle flour over the dough and roll the dough out to about ¼″ thickness and to fill the jellyroll pan. Dip cookie cutters in the flour and press them lightly into the dough just to make an indention. Use a butter knife to carve details or designs into the dough, making sure not to press too hard. In a small bowl, whisk together the egg yolks and water. Divide the egg yolk mixture into several small bowls and use a few drops of food coloring to create a different color in each bowl. Paint the cookie dough with the "paint". If the paint thickens, stir in a little water. Decorate the cookies with the small candies or chocolate chips. Bake the painted cookie scene in the preheated oven for about 17 minutes, or until the dough is light brown. Remove from oven and let cool for 10 minutes before cutting the big cookie into pieces.

Peanut Butter Ice Cream Sandwiches

Makes 18 sandwiches

36 peanut butter cookies
4½ C. chocolate or vanilla ice cream, slightly softened

Chopped peanuts or sprinkles, optional

For each ice cream sandwich, press about ¼ cup of the softened ice cream between 2 of the peanut butter cookies. Place on a jellyroll pan. Roll the ice cream edges in chopped peanuts or candies before freezing. Freeze about 30 minutes, until firm. To store, wrap sandwiches individually in plastic wrap. Let sit at room temperature a few minutes before serving. Any combination of cookies or ice cream can be used to make these sandwiches.

Berry Sundaes

Makes 4 servings

1 (16 oz.) pkg. fresh
  strawberries
1 (8 oz.) pkg. fresh
  raspberries
Sugar to taste

⅛ tsp. vanilla
2 C. vanilla ice cream
  or frozen yogurt
Fresh mint for garnish,
  optional

Remove the stems from the strawberries and slice, reserving 4 whole strawberries. In a food processor or blender, combine raspberries and sliced strawberries. Puree until smooth. Add sugar and vanilla and puree to mix. Scoop ice cream or frozen yogurt into 4 dessert bowls. Spoon berry sauce over ice cream. Top each bowl with one of the reserved whole strawberries and, if desired, garnish with a sprig of fresh mint.

Big Soft
Ginger Cookies

Makes 2 dozen

2¼ C. flour
2 tsp. ground ginger
1 tsp. baking soda
¾ tsp. cinnamon
½ tsp. ground cloves
¼ tsp. salt

¾ C. margarine, softened
1 C. plus 2 T. sugar, divided
1 egg
1 T. water
¼ C. molasses

Preheat oven to 350°. Into a large bowl, sift flour, ground ginger, baking soda, cinnamon, ground cloves and salt. In a separate large bowl, cream together margarine and 1 cup sugar, mixing until lightened and fluffy. Beat in egg and stir in water and molasses. Gradually stir in sifted ingredients and mix well. Shape tablespoonfuls of dough into rounded balls. Place remaining 2 tablespoons sugar in a shallow bowl. Roll balls in sugar and place, 2″ apart, onto ungreased baking sheets. Bake in oven for 8 to 10 minutes. Let cookies cool on baking sheet for 5 minutes before removing to a wire rack. Store in an airtight container.

Pumpkin Bars with Crumb Topping

Makes 10 to 12 servings

1½ C. quick cooking oats
1¼ C. flour
¾ C. plus ⅓ C. brown sugar, divided
½ C. chopped pecans or walnuts
½ tsp. salt

½ tsp. baking soda
¾ C. butter, softened
1 (16 oz.) can pumpkin puree
⅔ C. milk
1 egg
1 T. pumpkin pie spice

Preheat oven to 375°. In a large bowl, combine oats, flour, ¾ cup brown sugar, chopped pecans, salt, baking soda and softened butter. Beat until mixture is crumbly. Reserve about 1½ cups of the crumb mixture and press remaining mixture into a lightly greased 9 x 13″ baking dish. Bake in preheated oven for 10 minutes. To make filling, in a medium bowl, combine pumpkin puree, milk, remaining ⅓ cup brown sugar, egg and pumpkin pie spice. Beat until well blended and smooth. Spread filling over crust. Sprinkle reserved crumb mixture over top. Return to oven and bake for an additional 25 minutes. Remove from oven and let cool before cutting into bars.

Sugar Coated Pecans

Makes 3 cups

1 egg white	⅛ tsp. salt
1 C. brown sugar	1 tsp. vanilla
1 T. flour	3 C. pecans

    Preheat oven to 250°. In a medium bowl, whip egg white and slowly add brown sugar and flour. Add salt and vanilla. Fold in pecans. Lay covered pecans on a greased baking sheet and bake for about 45 minutes.

Caramel Popcorn

Makes 4 quarts

3 qts. popped popcorn
3 C. dry-roasted, unsalted
   mixed nuts
1 C. brown sugar
½ C. light corn syrup

½ C. margarine
½ tsp. salt
½ tsp. baking soda
½ tsp. vanilla

Preheat oven to 250°. In a large roasting pan, combine popped popcorn and nuts. Place in oven while preparing glaze. In a medium saucepan, combine brown sugar, corn syrup, margarine and salt. Remove from heat and stir in baking soda and vanilla. Pour glaze over warm popcorn and nuts, tossing to coat well. Bake another 60 minutes, stirring every 10 to 15 minutes. Cool and break apart. Store in an airtight container.

White Chocolate Crunch

Makes about 12 cups

2 lbs. white chocolate,
  coarsely chopped
6 C. crispy rice
  cereal squares
3 C. toasted oat cereal

2 C. thin pretzel sticks
2 C. cashews
1 (12 oz.) pkg.
  miniature M&M's

In a large double boiler over simmering water, place chopped white chocolate over medium heat, stirring until melted and smooth. In a large roaster pan or bowl, combine crispy rice cereal, toasted oat cereal, pretzel sticks, cashews and miniature M&M's. Pour the melted white chocolate over the mixture and carefully toss until well combined and evenly coated. Turn out onto waxed paper to cool. Store any leftovers in an airtight container. Many ingredients can be added or substituted to this mix, such as various nuts and other assorted small candies.

Puppy Chow

Makes about 9 cups

1 C. chocolate chips   1½ C. powdered sugar
½ C. creamy peanut butter
9 C. crispy rice
   cereal squares

In a large double boiler over simmering water, place chocolate chips. Heat, stirring often, until chocolate is completely melted. Add peanut butter and stir until smooth. Remove from heat. Add crispy rice cereal and stir until well coated. Pour powdered sugar into a large plastic bag. Add chocolate-coated cereal and shake until well coated. Store any leftover puppy chow in an airtight container.

Strawberry Freeze

Makes 18 servings

¾ C. sugar
1 (8 oz.) pkg. cream cheese, softened
1 (20 oz.) can crushed pineapple, drained

1 (10 oz.) pkg. frozen sliced strawberries, thawed
2 bananas, diced
1 (8 oz.) container frozen whipped topping, thawed

In a medium bowl, cream together sugar and cream cheese, mixing until smooth. In a separate bowl, combine crushed pineapple, thawed strawberries, diced bananas and whipped topping. Fold fruit mixture into cream cheese mixture and mix until evenly blended. Spread mixture into a 9 x 13″ baking dish. Cover with plastic wrap and freeze for 8 hours or overnight. Remove from freezer 20 minutes before cutting into squares and serving.

Lemon Cookies

Makes about 2 dozen

1 (18 oz.) pkg. lemon
   cake mix
1 egg

1 (8 oz.) container frozen
   whipped topping, thawed
Powdered sugar

    Preheat oven to 325°. In a large bowl, combine lemon cake mix, egg and whipped topping. Mix thoroughly until dough is sticky and stiff. Drop dough by teaspoonfuls into a small bowl of powdered sugar. Completely coat each cookie in powdered sugar and place on an ungreased baking sheet. Bake for no more than 8 to 10 minutes, being careful not to brown cookies. The cookies will be soft and crinkled on top when done. Immediately remove cookies from oven and let cool slightly on baking sheet before transferring to parchment paper or a wire rack to cool completely.

Chocolate Cinnamon Pudding

Makes 8 servings

½ C. sugar
2 T. cornstarch
1 tsp. cinnamon
2 (12 oz.) cans
 evaporated milk

1 C. chocolate chips
2 egg yolks, lightly beaten
½ C. shredded coconut

In a large saucepan over medium heat, combine sugar, cornstarch and cinnamon. Gradually stir in evaporated milk, chocolate chips and beaten egg yolks. Bring to a boil, stirring constantly, until mixture is thickened. Pour chocolate mixture into 8 individual serving cups. Chill in refrigerator for 1 hour. Sprinkle shredded coconut over each serving.

Crispy Caramel Treats

Makes 32 treats

4 Milky Way candy bars   3 C. crispy rice cereal
¾ C. butter or margarine,   1 C. milk chocolate chips
  divided

In microwave or a double boiler, melt candy bars and ½ cup butter, stirring occasionally, until smooth. Stir in crispy rice cereal until well coated. Press mixture into a greased 7 x 11″ pan. In a separate microwave-safe bowl or double boiler, melt chocolate chips and remaining ¼ cup butter, stirring until smooth. Remove from heat and spread chocolate mixture over ingredients in pan. Refrigerate 1 hour, or until firm. To serve, cut into small squares.

Honey Nut Cookies

Makes 4 dozen

16 graham crackers
1 C. crunchy peanut butter
⅔ C. honey

½ C. evaporated milk
1 C. shredded coconut

Crush the graham crackers in a food processor or between 2 pieces of waxed paper using a rolling pin. In a large mixing bowl, combine peanut butter, honey and evaporated milk. Mix well. Stir in crushed graham crackers. Make small balls with dough and place on waxed paper. Roll balls in shredded coconut and serve.

Mudslide Pie

Makes 8 servings

1 C. chocolate chips
1 tsp. instant coffee granules
1 tsp. hot water
¾ C. sour cream
½ C. sugar
1 tsp. vanilla
1 (9″) prepared chocolate
  crumb pie crust

1½ C. heavy whipping cream
1 C. powdered sugar
¼ C. cocoa powder
2 T. miniature
  chocolate chips

In a double boiler over low heat, place chocolate chips. Heat until chocolate is melted and smooth, stirring frequently. Remove from heat and let cool for 10 minutes. In a medium bowl, combine instant coffee granules and hot water. Add sour cream, sugar and vanilla and mix until sugar is completely dissolved. Stir in melted chocolate and mix until smooth. Spread mixture into prepared crust and chill in refrigerator. In a small mixing bowl, beat heavy whipping cream, powdered sugar and cocoa powder at high speed until stiff peaks form. Spread mixture over chilled chocolate layer in crust. Sprinkle miniature chocolate chips over pie and place in freezer for 6 hours or until firm.

Hawaiian Tarts

Makes 3 dozen

1 C. butter, softened
1 tsp. vanilla
½ C. plus ⅓ C. powdered
   sugar, divided
1¾ C. flour

2 T. cornstarch
1 C. pineapple preserves
½ C. sugar
1 egg
1½ C. shredded coconut

Preheat oven to 350°. In a large bowl, cream together butter, vanilla and ½ cup powdered sugar, mixing until smooth. Into a separate bowl, sift flour and cornstarch. Add sifted mixture to creamed mixture and stir until a dough forms. Roll dough into 1″ balls and press 1 ball into each cup of greased miniature muffin tins. Press dough onto bottom and up sides of muffin tins to form cups. Place 1 teaspoon pineapple preserves in each cup. In a small bowl, combine sugar and egg, mixing until well blended. Stir in shredded coconut. Place 1 teaspoon coconut mixture over pineapple in each cup. Bake in oven for 25 to 30 minutes, until slightly golden brown. Let tarts cool in pan for 15 minutes. Lightly tap the muffin tins on the counter to loosen tarts. Before serving, dust tarts with remaining ⅓ cup powdered sugar.

Easy Fruit Parfaits

Makes 4 servings

1 C. boiling water
1 (3 oz.) pkg. red gelatin,
  any flavor
1 C. cold water

1 (15¼ oz.) can tropical
  fruit salad, drained
Thawed whipped topping

In a medium bowl, combine boiling water and red gelatin, mixing until completely dissolved. Stir in cold water. Pour gelatin into 4 tall dessert or parfait glasses, filling about half full. Refrigerate filled glasses for 4 hours or until firm. To serve, layer whipped topping over gelatin and place tropical fruit over whipped topping.

Salted Nut Roll Bars

Makes 10 to 12 servings

1 (14 oz.) can sweetened
condensed milk
1 (12 oz.) pkg. peanut
butter chips

3 C. miniature marshmallows
2 (12 oz.) jars salted or dry
roasted peanuts, divided

In a microwave-safe bowl, combine sweetened condensed milk, peanut butter chips and marshmallows. Microwave for about 2½ minutes, until melted, stirring after every 30 seconds. Spread 1 jar of peanuts into a greased 9 x 13″ pan. Spread marshmallow mixture over peanuts. Top with remaining 1 jar of peanuts and press down lightly. Refrigerate for about 1 hour before cutting into bars.

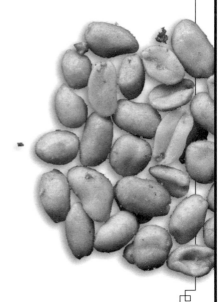

Gingerbread Family

4½ C. flour	½ C. butter, softened
1 T. cinnamon	½ C. brown sugar
2 tsp. ground ginger	2 eggs
1¼ tsp. baking soda	¾ C. molasses

In a large bowl, combine flour, cinnamon, ground ginger and baking soda. In a separate large bowl, cream together butter and brown sugar at medium speed until well combined. Add the eggs to the brown sugar mixture, one a time, beating well after each addition and stir in the molasses. Slowly add the dry mixture, stirring constantly. The dough will be stiff. Divide the dough in half and shape into small rectangles. Wrap the dough halves in plastic wrap and chill in refrigerator for 1 to 2 hours. Preheat oven to 350°. On a lightly floured flat surface, roll out half of the dough to about ¼″ thickness. Use a gingerbread person cookie cutter to cut the dough into shapes, or trace a cardboard template into the dough. Place the cut out shapes on an ungreased baking sheet and bake for about 10 minutes, or until the cookies are lightly browned. Remove from oven and let cool on baking sheets before transferring to wire racks to cool completely. Repeat with remaining dough. Use decorator's frosting, small candies and licorice to decorate the gingerbread family. Encourage everyone to decorate the cookies like members of the family. You could even include the pets!

Fun Camping Ideas

Group Storytelling

Instead of having one person do all the storytelling around the campfire, involve the entire family by telling a group story. One person starts the story and, at a good breaking point, that person chooses someone else to continue the story from that spot. The story may go something like this:

Storyteller 1: Once upon a time, there was a happy family who lived…

Storyteller 2: in a house that floated down the Purple Twisty River. They loved to eat…

Storyteller 3: popcorn and roast beef. One day…

Storyteller 4: the happy family's boat crashed into the rocks at one of the twistiest twists of the Purple River. They climbed on shore and…

Stargazing

For years, the stars have guided voyagers across land and water, inspired philosophers and grabbed the attention of many-a-romantic lover or dreamer. With some practice and a little orientation, the mysterious pictures in the night sky can become easier to spot. For best viewing conditions, go stargazing on a night that is clear, moonless and far from city lights. Be sure to pack a star chart and take a flashlight. Cover the flashlight with cellophane and secure with a rubber band. This will keep the light from being too bright but will still allow you to read the star chart.

The Big Dipper is probably the most-recognized constellation. It is believed that if you make a wish on the stars of the Big Dipper in the summer months that it will come true because the "ladle" of this constellation is facing up, so the wish can't fall out. The Big Dipper is part of a larger constellation called the Great Bear. The handle of the Big Dipper forms the bear's tail. The middle star on the handle has a very faint, tiny companion star that was used by ancient Arabs to test people's vision.

In addition to gazing at the more than 3,000 stars that are visible to the naked eye, you can also search for planets, which appear as star-like objects that do not twinkle. You may also see satellites, which move steadily and slowly across the sky. If you are lucky, you may be able to see a shooting star. You can explain that these are, in fact, not stars but actually chunks of metal and stone called meteors.

Flashlight Tag

This is a great game for after the sun goes down. To begin, divide the players into groups of two. Each group needs to create their own secret flashlight signal, for example; one short and one long flash, or three short flashes, etc. The two partners must then separate and go off in separate directions across a large open field or park area. The players are given one minute to scatter in different directions before they can begin flashing their secret signals. The first pair to reunite as quickly as possible by recognizing their secret signal is the winner. No talking allowed!

Free Association

This is a fun game that will get the entire family laughing. Someone starts the game by saying a word that is related to camping (or any topic) and then the next player has to say the first word that comes to mind. If no one can understand the connection between the words, then that player must explain why it was the first word to come to their mind. Continue playing until someone gets stuck and can't think of a word or everyone is rolling in laughter. Start over with a new word. The game might go something like this:

Player 1: Campfire

Player 2: Logs

Player 3: Trees

Player 4: Birds

Player 5: Feathers

Throwing The Smile

This is a fun game that will get everyone (even a grumpy camper) in a good mood. Have everyone sit in a circle around the campfire. Tell everyone that no smiling is aloud and everyone must sit with a somber look on their face until it is their turn. The object of the game is throw the smile around the group. Soon everyone won't be able to keep a straight face and smiling will abound!

Have one player start by making the biggest, happiest smile that they can. They have to hold it for 10 seconds before using their hand to wipe the smile from their face and throw it to someone else in the circle.

S'mores

Makes 1 serving

1 marshmallow   **½ Hershey's chocolate bar**
1 graham cracker

You will need matches and a long pointed stick. Build a campfire. Insert the marshmallow onto the end of the pointed stick. Hold the stick so the marshmallow is about 12″ to 15″ above the hot coals of the fire. Toast the marshmallow over the campfire to your desired doneness. Break the graham cracker in half and place the chocolate bar half on one of the crackers. Place the toasted marshmallow between the graham crackers to make a sandwich.

Sailor S'mores

Makes 1 serving

1 marshmallow   **¼ Hershey's chocolate bar**
Creamy peanut butter   **2 saltine crackers**

You will need matches, a butter knife and a long pointed stick. Build a campfire. Insert the marshmallow onto the end of the pointed stick. Hold the stick so marshmallow is about 12″ to 15″ above the hot coals of the fire. Toast the marshmallow over the campfire to your desired doneness. Use the butter knife to spread peanut butter onto one side of each saltine cracker and place the chocolate bar piece on one of the saltines. Place the toasted marshmallow between the saltines to make a sandwich.

Hawaiian Roasts

Makes 4 servings

**4 to 6 hot dogs,
  cut into pieces**

**1 (20 oz.) can pineapple
  chunks, drained**

You will need matches, a can opener and four long pointed sticks. Build a campfire. Have each camper slide the hot dog pieces and pineapple chunks onto their pointed stick. Hold the sticks about 8″ to 10″ above the hot coals of the fire. Cook until the hot dogs are heated throughout, about 5 to 8 minutes.

Little Smokie Sticks

Makes 4 servings

1 (16 oz.) pkg. lil'
  smokies wieners
4 dill pickles,
  cut into ¾″ pieces
1 pint cherry tomatoes
1 (4 oz.) can button
  mushrooms, drained

15 large pimiento-
  stuffed green olives
1 green bell pepper,
  cut into ¾″ squares

You will need matches, a sharp knife, a can opener and four long pointed sticks. Build a campfire. Have each camper build their kabobs by sliding the little smokies, pickle pieces, cherry tomatoes, button mushrooms, green olives and green bell pepper squares onto their pointed stick. Hold the kabobs about 8″ to 10″ above the hot coals. Cook until the little smokies are heated throughout, about 5 to 8 minutes.

Caramel Toasties

Makes 6 servings

6 wrapped caramel squares   **12 Ritz crackers**

You will need matches and six long pointed sticks. Build a campfire. Unwrap the caramel squares and insert one caramel onto the end of a pointed stick for each camper. Hold the stick so the caramel is about 12″ to 15″ above hot coals. Toast the caramel over the campfire just until softened, being careful not to melt the caramel completely. Place one caramel between two Ritz crackers to make a sandwich.

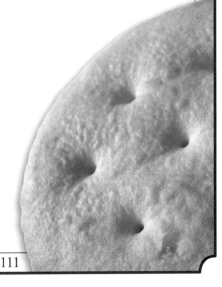

Hash Brown Pie

Makes 1 serving

1 C. frozen hash browns, thawed
½ C. chopped onions

1 tsp. garlic salt
Pepper to taste

You will need a pie iron, matches, a sharp knife, non-stick cooking spray, a medium bowl, a spoon and a hot pad. Build a flaming campfire. Generously grease both sides of the pie iron with non-stick cooking spray. In a medium bowl, combine the thawed hash browns, chopped onions and garlic salt. Mix well and season with pepper to taste. Pat the hash browns mixture into a square and set on one side of the pie iron. Close the pie iron and hold over flames for 8 to 10 minutes. Remove iron from fire and open carefully with a hot pad and remove the Hash Brown Pie.

Walking Tacos

Makes 4 servings

1 lb. prepared taco meat
½ C. shredded
  Cheddar cheese
Shredded lettuce

Chopped tomatoes
Sour cream
4 individual size bags Doritos

    You will need matches, a cast iron skillet, a spoon and four forks. Preheat the camping stove or place the grilling grate over a campfire. Place prepared taco meat in a cast iron skillet and place skillet over heat. Cook until taco meat is heated throughout. Open bags of Doritos and lightly crush the chips. Spoon heated taco meat into the bags and top with shredded Cheddar cheese, shredded lettuce, chopped tomatoes and sour cream. Eat walking tacos with a fork right from the bag.

Note: Prepare taco meat at home by browning
1 pound ground beef and mixing with ½ cup water and
1 envelope of taco seasoning. Pack in an airtight container and
place in cooler until ready to prepare recipe at the campsite.

Campin' Cowboy Casserole

Makes 5 servings

½ lb. bacon
1 lb. ground beef
1 small onion, chopped
2 (15 oz.) cans pork n' beans

⅓ C. barbecue sauce
1 tube of 10
  refrigerated biscuits

You will need matches, a cast iron skillet, paper towels, a sharp knife, a can opener and a cooking spoon. Preheat the camping stove or place the grilling grate over the campfire. Place bacon in a cast iron skillet and place skillet over heat. Cook bacon to desired crispness and remove from skillet to paper towels. When bacon has drained, crumble and set aside. Add ground beef and chopped onion to skillet and cook until ground beef is evenly browned and onions are tender. Drain grease from skillet and add crumbled bacon, pork n' beans and barbecue sauce. Bring mixture to a low boil. Separate tube into individual biscuits and place biscuits over ingredients in skillet. Cover skillet and let simmer for about 10 minutes, or until biscuits are golden brown. Place two biscuits on each plate and spoon casserole over biscuits.

Banana Boats

Makes 6 servings

6 large bananas
2 C. chocolate chips

1 (10 ½ oz.) pkg.
miniature marshmallows

You will need matches, a sharp knife, aluminum foil, long tongs, a hot pad and 6 spoons. Build a campfire. Set out six large pieces of aluminum foil. Leave the peels on the bananas, but remove the stems. Make a cut in each banana lengthwise from top to bottom. Spoon out a little of the banana flesh. Stuff the bananas with chocolate chips and marshmallows. Wrap each banana in aluminum foil. Place wrapped bananas directly in the coals of the campfire and cook for about 5 minutes, or until the chocolate is melted. Using long tongs, remove bananas from fire. Using a hot pad or oven mitt, slowly unwrap bananas. Eat banana boats with a spoon right from the peel.

Flamin' Pizza Pockets

Makes 2 servings

1 T. butter, softened
4 slices white bread
¼ C. pizza sauce
12 to 18 pepperoni slices

1 (4 oz.) can sliced
  mushrooms, drained
½ C. shredded
  mozzarella cheese

You will need a pie iron, matches, non-stick cooking spray, a butter knife, a can opener and a hot pad. Build a flaming campfire. Generously grease both sides of the pie iron with non-stick cooking spray. Spread butter over one side of each slice of bread. Place one slice of bread, buttered side out, into one side of the pie iron. Layer half of the pizza sauce, pepperoni slices, mushrooms and shredded mozzarella cheese onto the bread slice. Cover with another slice of bread, buttered side out. Close iron and hold over flames for 3 minutes on each side. Remove iron from fire and open carefully with a hot pad or oven mitt. Repeat with remaining ingredients.

Pineapple Upside Down Cake

Makes 2 servings

1 cake donut

2 pineapple rings

1 T. butter

4 tsp. brown sugar

You will need matches, a sharp knife, aluminum foil, long tongs and a hot pad. Build a campfire. Set out two large pieces of aluminum foil. Cut the cake donuts in half and set one half on each piece of foil. Lay one pineapple slice on each donut half and dot pineapple slices with butter. Sprinkle brown sugar over each slice. Wrap aluminum foil up around ingredients and seal tightly. Place wrapped cakes directly in the coals of the campfire and cook for about 10 to 15 minutes. Using long tongs, remove packets from the fire. Using a hot pad, slowly unwrap packets and enjoy the cake!

Fire Baked Apples

Makes 2 servings

**2 Granny Smith apples,
  cored**

**2 T. brown sugar
½ tsp. cinnamon**

You will need matches, an apple corer or sharp knife, aluminum foil, measuring spoons, long tongs, a hot pad and two forks. Build a campfire. Core the apples and fill the core of each apple with 1 tablespoon brown sugar and ¼ teaspoon cinnamon. Wrap each apple completely in a large piece of aluminum foil, twisting the extra foil at the top to make a handle. Place wrapped apples directly in the coals of the campfire and cook for 5 to 10 minutes, until softened. Using long tongs, remove the apples from the fire. Using the hot pad, slowly unwrap the apples, being careful not to spill any hot sugar. Eat the baked apples with a fork.

Grilled Potato Wedges

Makes 3 to 4 servings

2 to 3 large potatoes, washed and scrubbed	**½ tsp. dried thyme**
	½ tsp. dried oregano
1 T. olive oil	**Salt and pepper to taste**

You will need matches, aluminum foil, a sharp knife and a basting brush. Cover the grate of the grill with aluminum foil. Preheat the grill or place the grilling grate over a campfire. Cut potatoes into ⅓″ to ½″ wedges. Brush potato slices with olive oil and sprinkle with dried thyme and dried oregano. Lay potato wedges over aluminum foil on the grill. Sprinkle with salt and pepper to taste. Grill wedges to desired tenderness, turning occasionally.

The Best Corn on the Cob

Makes 4 servings

4 ears of corn
1½ T. butter, melted
½ tsp. ground cumin

¼ tsp. chili powder
1 tsp. fresh chopped cilantro

You will need matches, a small bowl, a spoon, measuring spoons and a basting brush. Preheat grill or place grilling grate over campfire. Pull back husks from ears of corn, leaving the husks attached. Remove 1 strip of husk from the inner side of each ear of corn and set aside. In a small bowl, combine melted butter, ground cumin, chili powder and chopped cilantro. Brush melted butter mixture onto the corn. Bring husks up to cover corn and tie husks together with reserved strips of husk. Place corn cobs on the hot grate and grill for 20 to 30 minutes, turning corn occasionally.

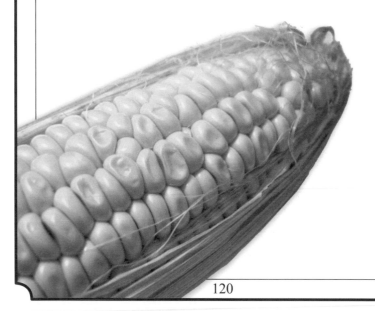

Index

──────── **Fun Camping Ideas** ────────